COTTINGHAM SCHOOLS IN THE NINETEENTH CENTURY

A Study of a Yorkshire Village Community

by Peter Railton

HUTTON PRESS

1986

Published by the Hutton Press Ltd
130 Canada Drive, Cherry Burton, Beverley
East Yorkshire HU17 7SB

Phototypeset in 11 on 12 point Times Roman
and Printed by
The Walkergate Press Limited
Lewis House, Springfield Way, Anlaby, Hull HU10 6RX

ISBN 0 907033 46 6

CONTENTS

LIST OF ILLUSTRATIONS

ACKNOWLEDGEMENTS

The Author wishes to thank the following for their assistance in the writing of this book:

Mr. Albert Barker, for his early memories of the Hallgate School.

Miss Dales for information regarding Frances Coupland's School in Church House.

The late Mr. J. Gibson, for family details of his grandparents, Mr. and Mrs. A. B. Moorby.

Mr. 'Dick' Grantham, for his recollections of the King Street rooms.

Mr. and Mrs. Kenneth Green for their generous help with photographic and other material.

Mr. P. Hassam, retired former Headmaster of the Hallgate School, for help with old School Log Books.

Mrs. Jones, for her early memories of the Hallgate Infants' School.

John Lawson, Reader Emeritus in Educational Studies, University of Hull, for dates of Cottingham teachers in the 17th Century.

Miss Kit Raper, for her memories of private schools and the early days of the Hallgate School.

Mr. H. R. Wright, a Governor of Hallgate School and a member of the Cottingham Parochial Church Council, for some material on the National School.

Mr. W. L. Wright, retired former teacher at the Hallgate School, for his personal recollections.

The anonymous donors of the old photographs of pupils and staff of the Cottingham Board Schools and of Eastholme College.

Mr. K. D. Holt, the County Archivist, Humberside County Record Office, Beverley, and his staff for the facilities extended.

The Librarian of the Local Studies Library, Hull Central Library, and the Archivist of the Kingston upon Hull Record Office, and their staff for services provided.

Peter Railton
Cottingham
September 1986

INTRODUCTION

The village of Cottingham lies five miles north west of the city of Kingston upon Hull and is reputed to be the largest village in England. Cottingham was known as a manor at the time when Domesday book was compiled. The name Cot-Ing-Ham implies Saxon origins, Ing or Ings being an area of land and Ham a settlement; Cot may be a derivative of the name of the chief of the settlement or a reference to the Saxon deity Kot or Kit. In Leland's 'Collectonea' it is noted that William d'Estateville or Stuteville being Sheriff of Yorkshire, entertained King John at his house in the village and in 1200 obtained a licence to hold a market and fairs and to fortify his castle. Thus Cottingham can claim to have attracted Royal favour earlier than Hull. The medieval period left Cottingham with the beautiful parish church of St. Mary the Virgin, two priories and a castle. Unfortunately only the Church survives today.

There are records of schoolmasters teaching at Cottingham during the seventeenth century. In 1624 Thomas Martyn and Thomas Stainton taught as unlicensed schoolmasters. In 1627 Matthew Haggard BA arrived. Subscription Books record that in 1666 William Scott was teaching in the village; 1670 Stephen Clarke and in 1676 John Taylor.

This survey of educational provision in Cottingham deals with the nineteenth century and is of a general nature, concerned more with the types of school in existence rather than examining the provision of places within the schools. The village was fairly representative of the national pattern of schools. There were private schools; an endowed English Free School; a National School; a Wesleyan School; and a Board School.

In 1801 the population of the parish was 1,927 souls and covered 9,735 acres of very fertile land devoted to mixed farming and specialising in the production of fresh vegetables for the population of Hull. The population rose steadily up to the middle of the

7

century then it accelerated rapidly as can be seen in the appendix. The decade 1881-1891 saw an increase of about 4,000 souls and between 1891 and 1901 an increase of a further 6,000. These large increases are accounted for not only by a natural increase in the population of the village, but by influxes of people moving out of the City of Hull. As trade prospered it became fashionable for the better-off to move to the 'suburbs' and Cottingham with its rail link to town and improved roads was very popular. The age of the commuters had arrived! This tendency is still apparent today; Cottingham is still a popular place in which to live.

Cottingham can be said to be a microcosm of the educational expansion going on throughout the country in the last century. This was prompted by several factors. The pace of the Industrial Revolution taking place in the latter half of the 18th century quickened during the first half of the 19th. The population of the towns grew fast; that of the countryside declined. Along with this massive shift of population from countryside to town went attendant problems of house shortage and sanitation which quickly created social and medical problems. In response to this, medical science took big strides forward in finding and dealing with problems of environmental health. At the same time more and better food became available to more people able to afford it. Although cholera and various other diseases took their toll, the general tendency was toward a better standard of living for more people. Perhaps the biggest single factor in the population explosion was the fall in the infant mortality rate. This, coupled with better food, better housing and increased medical knowledge caused tremendous pressures, not the least of which was on education.

Throughout the country there existed a hotch-potch of educational establishments, from 'Dame schools' where an old lady would teach a few children for pennies to buy food with; an assortment of larger private schools; Charity Schools of various sizes endowed by a philanthropist for the benefit of poor or orphaned children; Free Schools, again endowed by a rich personage, the rents from land or property going toward the salary of a master or mistress to instruct 'deserving' pupils; Grammar Schools often long established but of varying degrees of efficiency; and Sunday Schools where the main object was to keep the young off the streets and direct their attentions to useful knowledge on their one day away from work.

It was the success of many of these Sunday Schools which prompted the Churches to extend Sunday teaching to weekday teaching. This was facilitated by several important Factory Acts which successively reduced the hours of working children and at the same time imposed lower age limits on working children.

Anglican and Nonconformists alike agreed that measures should be taken to deal with the growing pool of children on the streets. This gave rise to the founding of schools by the Anglican 'National Society for Promoting the Education of the Poor in the Principles of the Established Church' on the one hand and by the 'British and Foreign School Society' of the Nonconformists on the other. So in the early years of the 19th century denominational schools opened whose aim it was to teach reading, writing and numbers along with religious instruction. As the century wore on, the Societies received grants from the then Board of Education in London with which to maintain their schools, while at the same time pupils were charged a few pence for instruction. The Societies each had teacher training facilities; monitors, the older and brighter pupils, received personal instruction from the teacher and they then taught the younger children. This grew later into the pupil-teacher system.

Cottingham had representative schools of the two Societies as we shall see later. As Cottingham's population expanded rapidly toward the end of the century, so did the population at large. The Societies could not keep pace with the demand for more school places, so the 1870 Education Act set up School Boards in all areas whose responsibility it was to examine the provision of schools and where necessary build schools. These were to be undenominational, paid for by rates gathered locally and to be in receipt of government grant aid based upon the attainment of pupils' 'standards'. Our Hallgate Junior School is the representative of the School Board locally.

Throughout this period of change however, the private schools were still providing teaching for smaller numbers of children of parents who could afford the fees. We start our survey of Cottingham's Schools in the 19th century with the Private Schools.

9

PRIVATE SCHOOLS

In the columns of the *Hull Advertiser* during the last century are numerous notices of private schools in Cottingham catering for children of parents who could afford to pay the often high fees demanded even for those days. For example the Reverend W. Harding who was curate of Skidby lived at Cottingham and announced that he

> 'has taken a convenient house for the accommodation of a limited number of pupils, whom he intends to instruct in the Latin and Greek languages, writing and arithmetic. Parents or Guardians who may wish to commit their children to his care may depend upon every exertion being used, which may tend to promote their learning, morals and happiness. Terms: Forty-five guineas per annum. Entrance Two guineas. Washing Two guineas. NB The number will be kept to six'.[1]

There are many such adverts in the *Hull Advertiser* couched in the quaint expressive style of the period and reminiscent of Dickens, the Brontës or Jane Austen. The Reverend Harding's teaching was ambitious and similar to the curriculum of a grammar school, offering as it did Latin and Greek. There are many examples of these clergy-run schools or academies up and down the country. Sometimes they existed out of scholarly interest and sometimes in order to augment the stipend. Other examples of schools conducted by clergymen in Cottingham are those of the Rev. A. Kidd, who in June 1812 was offering to board four pupils in his own house and instruct them for the fee of forty guineas a year and extra for washing; the Rev. H. Benn in May 1829 who appraised the inhabitants of his intention to open a boarding school and day school at 'Willow Cottage', with what success is not known.

The Rev. James Deans was vicar of St. Mary's Church, Cottingham from 1808 until his death in 1832. He became Master at the Mark Kirby Free School and at the same time was teaching a

1 Cottingham Local History Society Journal, Vol. 2.

few boys privately in 1823. This private teaching was presumably undertaken in the rectory which, it is understood, was located at that time where a supermarket and estate agency now stand, on the corner of Hallgate and King Street (north). Incidentally, this part of King Street down to Northgate was formerly known as Broad Lane. The rectory opposite the church which was demolished and replaced by infant school buildings in recent years, was occupied by the Rev. Charles Overton during his 48 years as incumbent and was the successor of the older rectory occupied by James Deans and his wife Penelope. They had six children, four boys and two girls, all born between 1809 and 1817. If James' pupils were all boarders, his wife must have been kept very busy, although she might have had help in the house. His memorial stone can be seen just inside the chancel of St. Mary's, though it is very faded. It also records the death in infancy of one of his daughters, Penelope. James left in his will £200 for the benefit of the clergy of St. Mary's Church.

Not all the private schools were for boys. A Miss Alice Laverack began advertising in the *Hull Advertiser* at frequent intervals. In April 1815 she moved from Market Weighton to Cottingham and

William Green's School 'The Shrubbery', later renamed 'Northgate House'; the 'Northgate House' flats now occupy the site in Northgate, Cottingham

11

opened a 'Seminary for Young Ladies'. She took a 'large and commodious house' which at the time had already served as an 'Academy for Young Gentlemen', being the former school run by William Green, Esq. in King Street, who had moved his establishment into Northgate (see later).

Miss Laverack's terms were: Entrance fee one guinea. Board, English, plain and ornamental needlework 20 guineas per annum. Writing and arithmetic two guineas a year extra. Geography, with use of the globe (!), one guinea extra. French, Music and Drawing were all extras. The inevitable washing was two and a half guineas a year extra and,

> 'Young ladies should bring with them – 1 pair of sheets, 2 pillow cases, towels, table spoon, tea spoon – the spoons would be returned when the young ladies left the Seminary'.[2]

Miss Laverack appears to have moved to another house in 1821 and in 1822 she announced that a Miss Wimberley of Doncaster, an ex-governess, was taking over the school. By this time the seminary had moved yet again into Northgate. The fees had risen. Up to age 14, girls paid 20 guineas per year. After age 14 twenty-two guineas, but Board, English, Needlework, Geography (with globe!) were included. Miss Wimberley introduced Ancient and Modern History, also painting on glass and materials.

The school changed hands once more, for a Miss Dagget began advertising with herself as proprietress on the 3rd January, 1824. Her terms were lower – entrance fee ten shillings and six pence, then 16 guineas per year for board and instruction for pupils of ten years and under; 18 guineas thereafter. Shortly after this, no more advertisements appear so it seems that the Seminary ceased to function. Private schools were, by and large, temporary affairs. Much depended on the ability of the proprietor and on the confidence of the parents. Some advertised for only a short time. A Miss Lamb announced that her

> 'Establishment for a limited number of Young Ladies will be reopened on the 26th instant'.[3]

Her address is unknown. On 3rd April, 1835 Mrs. Tinkler notified the public that her school situated in George Street 'had vacancies for a limited number of Young Ladies'. On 30th June, 1843 Mrs. Croudace of Market Green thanked the public for their continued

2 *Hull Advertiser,* April 1815.
3 *Hull Advertiser,* 5th January, 1832.

12

support. In 1823 there were six private schools in Cottingham; in 1830 five; in 1840 six.[4]

By 1846 eight academies existed, but only two of the proprietors names listed in 1840 appear in 1846, such was the transitory nature of most private establishments. Several school owners seem to have combined the running of a school with another occupation. For example Wm. H. Carr was an assistant overseer of the poor and teacher at the Mark Kirby Free School; James Darling combined his school duties with those of Parish Clerk.

In 1855 another school appeared down George Street, administered by Susan and Elisabeth Wildish. Elisabeth Pickard had a school on Market Green. Did these ladies take over from the former occupiers of schools in George Street and Market Green respectively? It is almost impossible to say, but schools certainly did change hands whilst still being located at the same address.

In January, 1822 Thomas Stather reopened his academy after the Christmas vacation, prepared to instruct young gentlemen in

> 'all branches of useful Science. Terms: 18 guineas per annum. English Language, pronunciation, writing, arithmetic, history, composition, geography, maps, surveying and book-keeping. French, Latin, drawing, music or Greek six guineas a year extra'.[5]

Mr. Stather advertised for a Classics teacher in January and April 1826. His last advert appeared in December 1827.

There is some evidence to suggest that Stather occupied the building in King Street which had housed the seminary of Alice Laverack. He then moved into Thwaite Street.

There were two schools in the area of St. Mary's, apart from the Mark Kirby school. One was in the Churchyard and was an infants' school, shown on a surveyor's map of 1855 and having been built in 1830 to accommodate 16 pupils at a cost of £21.15.6½ d. This was on the front of Hallgate, opposite the gateway recently enlarged for vehicle access at the Council School, and directly in front of the church chancel. No visible evidence remains today, except an absence of gravestones earlier than the 1870's. There seems to be conflicting information regarding the administration of the school; one source indicates that it was probably built as a Church-run school; yet another believes that it had an endowment and was

4   Hull Directory, 1840.
5   Cottingham Local History Society, Vol. I.

transferred to the National Society as its infant department (See later chapter). Whatever the truth of it, it was being taught as an infant school in 1855 by a Miss Mary Ann Rawson.[6]

At the same time, 1855, there existed a small school in part of Church House. This is situated between the Mark Kirby School and Arlington Hall and housed part of the former workhouse until about 1840. There is an interesting inscription high up on the wall regarding its origins. The school was at the end nearest to Arlington Hall and was held on the ground floor. This was Frances Coupland's private school. The present occupier of Church House remembers her father speaking of it and of Miss Coupland still being there in the late 1880's.

In 1858 seven private schools existed; this must have been the peak, for in 1867 the number had dropped to four.[7]

The school with the longest history was that conducted by William Green and his family for over 40 years. It must have been in operation before 5th July, 1806, on which date William gave notice of its reopening on the 14th of that month.

In all probability the school was the one referred to earlier, prior to the building being taken over by Alice Laverack in 1815 and then by Thomas Stather in 1822 and situated in King Street. William's fees were one guinea for entry, two guineas a year for washing and mending and twenty guineas a year for board and education. Day scholars were also taken for a guinea a quarter. The curriculum included reading, writing, English grammar, arithmetic, book-keeping and geography.

William married a Miss Theodosia Pycock of Sculcoats in 1807. In 1810 he acquired several acres of agricultural land in Northgate – a good example of a schoolmaster 'diversifying' in case the number of pupils declined and rendered the keeping of a school uneconomic. Presumably William would employ people to work his land, as he was always referred to as a 'Schoolmaster' or 'Independent' or a 'Gentleman' in documents of the time. More land was added in 1825. He owned a pond and embankment opposite the north end of the present West End Road – the site is a grassy area next to a detached house and is part of the Hull University Hall of Residence 'The Lawns'. This was probably part of the original outer moat and embankment of Cottingham Castle.

6   Victoria County History, East Riding, Vol. 4.
7   Hull & District Directory, 1867.

The land extended back to the present Park Lane and included a plantation there. William also had interests in two houses, a brewery and a maltkiln in Broad Lane, the present King Street (north); and he owned two cottages and a garden in Hallgate on a corner near the church.

He appears to have been in his new school premises in Northgate in the early 1800's and to have let his old premises in King Street to Miss Alice Laverack of Market Weighton. William still owned his old school premises in the late 1830's but they were serving as a shop, house and outbuildings and were situated where the large block of flats, 'Elm Tree Court', now stands, just past the vehicle entrance to the flats and the Post Office, towards Newgate Street and close by the site of what was to become the National School (See later chapter). He sold them in 1842.

William Green's Academy in Northgate must have been one of the finest schools of the time in this area. It stood opposite the end of Broad Lane (King Street north), alongside the Cross Keys Inn which still occupies the same site. The house and some outbuildings were still standing until recent times, a fine example of Georgian

'Ryedale Villa', Hallgate. Used for a time as a private school.

15

architecture, and were occupied latterly by Dr. Sissons. The house was named 'Northgate House', as are the flats which now occupy the site, but in William's time the house was named 'The Shrubbery'. There were two distinct sets of buildings; there was a

'Commodious dwelling and School premises being a Garden and Playground, Coach House, Stable, Cowshed and two acres of land.

The house consists of Drawing room, Dining room, Breakfast room, Servants' Hall, large Kitchen, Housekeeper's room, Pantry, Back Kitchen, Dairy, Outhouses. Four family bedrooms and four large bedrooms suitable for Boarders'.[8]

It became a 'Classical and Commercial Boarding School' in 1819; Latin, Greek and French were added to the curriculum which was

'requisite to qualify Youth to fill with respectability the various Departments in Business and Mercantile Life'.[9]

The latter reference is significant in view of the growing importance of Hull as port and city.

William and Theodosia had four children, three boys and one girl. William born in 1810, George in 1811, Theodosia in 1814 and James in 1816. They were a non-conformist family. In January 1832 William was advertising his Classical and Commercial Boarding School at Cottingham being conducted by 'William Green and Sons', so presumably at least two of his sons were active in teaching up to 1836, when no more references are made to them.

In April, 1837 William denied rumours that his school was to close, perhaps due to his sons being no longer involved and because of the threat to day pupil numbers posed by the opening of the National School in January 1836 (See later). However, in November, 1837 he gave notice of his intention to dispose of the premises

'so eligible for a Boarding School or residence for a genteel family. The house of ample size, the School Room spacious and airy with an excellent Playground and garden'.[10]

The premises were taken by a Mr. Peche, who hoped the parents who had favoured Mr. Green with their offspring would do the same for him. Evidently they did not do so for long because in July, 1840 Miss Theodosia Green advertised for six young ladies as

8   *Hull Advertiser,* July, 1849.
9   *Hull Advertiser,* January, 1819.
10 *Hull Advertiser,* November, 1837.

boarders; the school being the one formerly administered by her father and brothers. This can not have been a success either, for in July, 1842 William informed the public of his intention to reopen as Proprietor and employing a Mr. Cranmer as a tutor. The subjects taught were similar to those included earlier, but the fees were 30 guineas a year inclusive of washing.

Then in March, 1848 the following notice appeared:

'To Schoolmasters: To be disposed of, a school in the neighbourhood of Hull now in full practice. The fixtures etc. to be taken at a fair valuation. Apply at the office of this paper'.[11]

William found a tenant for the school within a short time:

'Classical and Commercial Boarding and Day School, Cottingham. Mr. W. G. Plees, Assistant Master at Kingston College, begs to inform the Gentry and the Public Generally of Cottingham, Hull and their vicinities; that he has taken the house and premises in which Mr. Green has for many years carried on a school at Cottingham, where he intends to open a Classical and Commercial Boarding and Day School and hopes by assiduous attention to the comforts, improvements and welfare of his pupils, to obtain a share of public patronage and support'.[12]

Mr. Plees cannot have had the 'share of public patronage and support' that he wanted, for in August 1849 the premises were put up for sale.

'The situation presents peculiar advantages for a school, from the number of respectable Families residing in the village, and from its being within a few minutes Railroad Distance from Hull and Beverley'.[13]

A sale of school furniture and effects was also held, indicating that after some 40 years the school administered by William Green and his family, and latterly by two other schoolmasters was ended. However, the building's association with children was not completely finished because a kindergarten was held in part of the old school building on the right of the house in the photograph (Page 11).

It is interesting to note that just as William's old school premises in King Street were at the back of the National School, his

11 *Hull Advertiser*, 24th March, 1848.
12 *Hull Advertiser*, 28th June, 1848.
13 *Hull Advertiser*, 27th July, 1849.

Northgate premises were next door to what was to become the Wesleyan Chapel and School situated where the Salvation Army building and Cottingham Rifle Club now stand (See later). A narrow public footpath separates the sites of these two old schools.

The census of 1841 shows that there were nine schoolmasters or schoolmistresses listed by name in Cottingham. William Green and his daughter Theodosia were at their premises in Northgate. Frances Coupland, who had her school in Church House, lived in Northgate. William H. Carr, teacher at the Mark Kirby School, private schoolmaster and overseer of the poor, also lived in Northgate. Elisabeth Kosk was down George Street. Mitchell Green and his wife Ann and their three children lived in Hallgate; it is not known if Mitchell was related to William Green and his family – at any rate he was not one of William's sons. Elisabeth Pratt lived in Beck Bank. Garvis Taylor and his wife Sarah and their three children lived in Brunswick Place, King Street. John Morton was in Broad Lane – the present King Street (north). Mary Scruton's address was Clough Road, then in the parish of Cottingham.

Some of the above are known to have kept a school themselves while others, presumably, were employed in the larger private schools or in the service of the National School (See later).

Two private schools existing late in the last century are within living memory. In 1891 Miss Kit Raper, now a remarkable centenarian, started at Miss Lawn's school in Hallgate. The fees were ten shillings and sixpence a quarter and evidently a good grounding was given. The school was housed in 'Rydale Villa' (see photograph on page 15), which is now a bank, but the upper part of the building remains unaltered. Miss Lawn's family were in business in Cottingham and it was often the case that a young lady of such a family was either a governess or kept a small school. A similar situation existed at the school Miss Raper attended next.

This was kept by a Miss Merrikin in Finkle Street. The Merrikins were business people and lived at Bondyke House on the corner of Southwood Road and St. Margaret's Avenue. Miss Merrikin had worked in Africa as a missionary and upon her return home set up a school. This was held in one of the cottages which stood between the present Darby and Joan Club and the corner of Market Green. Her terms were similar to Miss Lawn's. The pupils sat at desks and wrote and drew in exercise books. Only the infants used slates. Miss Raper believes that there were about twelve pupils in the school and probably about the same number at Miss Lawn's. Miss Raper admits to being a bit of a dare-devil; at the instigation of another pupil she made the excuse of going to the toilet which was outside at the back of the school. Instead, she ran across into King Street and up to a greengrocer's shop which stood near the present optician's premises, close to the corner of King Street and Newgate Street. She snatched a cabbage leaf and ran back to school, triumphantly thrusting the cabbage leaf into the hand of her surprised friend!

The curriculum was the usual one of reading, writing, arithmetic, nature and poetry which was becoming more popular at this time. There is now no evidence as to the quality of instruction in the earlier private schools in Cottingham, but the schools conducted by Miss Lawn and Miss Merrikin respectively set very high standards.

A larger private school in Cottingham toward the end of the last century was 'Eastholme College' in Hallgate. This was administered by the Misses Lucy and Annie Elizabeth Lister and was located in two adjoining houses, numbers 22 and 24 which have

'Eastholme College', Hallgate, about 1900.

19

remained largely unaltered externally to the present time (see photograph). The school appears in many local Directories from the 1880's until the early years of this century. Boys as well as girls were taught by the Miss Listers, who had a staff of several teachers; also pupil teachers who taught the younger children and eventually became teachers themselves. The school catered for boarders as well as day pupils, some boarders coming from other counties, such was the reputation of 'Eastholme College'.

A former pupil remembers a Mr. Porter coming to the school to teach singing and a French lady taken on to the staff to teach French. The pupils had uniforms. Girls wore pale blue skirts and jackets and white hats with a matching pale blue ribbon around them. The boys had blue uniforms also.

A high cultural standard was the aim of the school. The Miss Listers were greeted with 'Bonjour Madame' at the start of each day in school. Each lunchtime weather permitting, the boarders were taken for a walk. They were expected to behave with the decorum befitting the College, walking in pairs, crocodile fashion, through the village. There were about a hundred pupils at this school in its heyday, which offered not only a good education but also sound training in the social graces.

Almost opposite 'Eastholme' is a block of very tall houses known as 'Arlington Villas'. There was a school in one of these, run by a Miss Gale. It was a very much smaller affair altogether, catering for a few day pupils but of a good standard. The school was contemporaneous with 'Eastholme' and some children were sent there first as infants before proceeding to the larger establishment across the road later.

'Eastholme' had a successor in more recent times; there was also a very prestigious College for boys down Northgate, but these fall outside the self-imposed limiting date of 1904 and hopefully will be dealt with in a later work.

This survey of Cottingham's private schools is mirrored in similar schools all over the country. The fortunes of the schools fluctuated as the numbers of pupils did. Schools closed as numbers fell or opened as demand rose. The *Victoria County History of York, East Riding* tells us that in Cottingham in 1819 several small schools had, altogether, 170 pupils out of a total population of just over 2,000 people. In 1833 pupils numbers had risen to 205 out of a population of 2,500.

What the quality of teaching was like in the earlier private schools is largely unknown. This was in the days before any large scale training of professionally qualified teachers. No doubt the clergy would seek to instruct their pupils in a responsible manner, as would other enthusiastic individuals, male and female, many of whom saw it as their christian duty to help in the instruction of children. It is also probably true to say that in keeping with the country generally, some private schools were simply child-minding establishments.

However, there is no doubt that many private schools both large and small played a very important part in the education of Cottingham's children. The education they received could lead to university or a business careeer – without the private schools many children would have gone without instruction altogether up to the advent of the denominational schools in the village. It is perhaps significant that 31 years after the establishment of the National School which offered cheap education, there were four private schools still open, almost certainly charging high fees. This indicates that there were parents, who for various reasons, were willing to pay for their children to attend a private school then, as there are now. Pupils usually started school at five or six years old; some went right through while others left to go elsewhere – or just left. Attendance at any school was not compulsory until 1880 and even then was not easy to enforce.

Toward the end of the century many children left their school and started at the newly opened Cottingham Board School at ten or eleven years of age. In the earlier years of the century the denominational schools were often the recipients, or the Mark Kirby School, to which we must now turn.

MARK KIRBY FREE SCHOOL

'Mark Kirby by will dated 16th September, 1712 devised the yearly rents and profits of a close of meadow in Cottingham, called Paradise, with three storey of meadow in the Inglemire, a turf pit or garth in the common, and two gates in the Firth, to be paid yearly to the schoolmaster of the school in Cottingham Church Yard, commonly called the Free School, and to his successors, for teaching ten poor children of parents not of ability to pay for their learning, such children to be appointed and approved of by his heir's, the minister and churchwardens of Cottingham, the said schoolmaster and their successors, or any two of them, whereof his heir to be one; and he further devised, after the death of Mary Levitt, widow, the rents of a close or garth purchased by him of Thomas Trevis unto the said schoolmaster and his successors forever, for the purposes aforesaid; and he directed, that the premises should be let for no longer term than one year, and so from year to year, by his heirs, the said Minister, churchwardens and schoolmaster, for the time being, or by any two of them whereof his heir to be one. The heir at law of the testator is Sir Mark Masterman Sykes Bart'.[1]

The mastership of the free school at Cottingham referred to in this will was under the appointment of the lord of the manor of Cottingham. The free-school seems to have been founded originally by John Wardel late in the 17th century.

The Kirbys were prominent people in Hull. In Hadley's *History of Hull, 1788* a reference is made to 'a sumptuous monument of Mark Kirby and his family' in Holy Trinity Church.

'The free school appears to be of considerable antiquity; but it is endowed with no other property than that derived under the will of Mark Kirby and there appears to be no obligation on

1   *Reports of the Commissions on Charities and Education – York and the East Riding, 1815-1839.*

the master, by usage, to teach gratuitously more than the ten scholars for whose education provision is made by the will'.[2]

Mark Kirby had an estate at Sledmere but was born at Cottingham hence the interest in the village. At the time of the Charity Commission's report referred to, the property derived under the will consisted of the 'Paradise Close' of six acres, and another close of ten acres in Cottingham Ings Common which was allotted on an enclosure in lieu of the other property mentioned in the will. The letting of the land was left by the trustees and heir of the founder to the schoolmaster and he was letting the closes to a John Stevenson, as a yearly tenant.

The Mark Kirby Free School had a very chequered existence. Disputes between the trustees and the Master or the trustees and the Church seem to have been a dominant feature. In the 18th century the appointment of a schoolmaster had to be made by the Church – usually by the Vicar General of the diocese in which the school was situated. A copy of a letter was featured in the Journal of Cottingham Local History Society concerning a dispute between rival claimants for the post of schoolmaster, a Thomas Stow and an Isaac Southeren.

> '*Mr. Jubb,*
>
> *The bearer (Thomas Stow) comes for a Licence to teach Publick Schoole of Cottingham, having mine and the whole Parish consent and approbacion. He had some thoughts of removeing into Holderness, but being otherwise resolved he designs to fix here and he requests to have the Chancellor's Licence in order to suppress Isaac Southeren whom I mentioned to you some time since. I beg you will please get him dispatcht at the earliest charge.*
>
> *Sir,*
> *Your very humble servant*
> *Walter Hickson*
> *Nov. 4th 1717.*[3]

The Reverend Walter Hickson was the Vicar of Cottingham at the time and Mr. Jubb was the Diocesan official. It is not clear whether Stow and Southeren were both seeking the post at the Free School or whether Stow with the support of the Vicar was seeking an injunction to stop Southeren teaching privately.

2   ibid p.742.
3   *Journal of Cottingham Local History Society, January 1956,* Vol. I p.58-9.

In 1785, the sum of £100 was given by N. C. Burton, Esq., the Lord of the Manor, for providing a schoolhouse for the Master but the money was applied towards enlarging the parish workhouse and the master was given rooms in that building. Apparently the Lord of the Manor disputed with the Parish the right to nominate the schoolmaster. William Hardy was installed in his room above the workhouse and then given notice to quit by the Parish. He refused to go so he was forcibly ejected. He and Mr. Burton appealed to law and the case was heard at York. The trial lasted ten days and cost over £300 and this meant a rate of 1s. 2d. in the pound for the Parish to bear, as against rate of 4d. in the previous year, to pay for the litigation. It was reported that four Overseers of the Poor and twenty-five witnesses climbed aboard Robert Coverdale's wagon to journey to York to give evidence. Hardy was reinstated in his appointment forthwith.

In 1808 William Hardy died having held the position for forty-one years. Shortly afterwards, the Vicar, the Rev. James Deans became master and for the first four years of his mastership taught the pupils himself, later delegating his duties to a curate. At this time the number of children taught in the school had risen and fluctuated between ten and twenty. At the time of the Charity Commission Report 1815-1839, the number was fourteen. This was probably sometime in the second decade of the 19th century, as the Commissioners refer to the Rev. Deans, and he died in 1832.

The children were instructed in arithmetic, reading and writing. Several other children were fee-payers. The fourteen referred to were children educated free through the will of Mark Kirby. The free scholars were usually appointed by the master with the advice or consent of the church-wardens. The heir-at-law of the donor did not interfere in the choice. According to Archbishop Herring's Visitation returns for 1743 the school was an 'English School', offering education as above and appropriate for boys hoping to become apprenticed tradesmen or clerks. Mark Kirby's will repeatedly refers to 'scholars' – but records refer to 'boys', indicating parental attitudes that boys needed educating as the potential wage-earners later.

The Charity Commissioners were critical of the fact that the master, the Rev. James Deans, delegated the responsibility of the teaching to his curate,

'The master is sensible that his duty requires him to instruct the scholars himself; but in extenuation of his neglect of that duty it is represented on his side that on the appointment of a deputy he stipulated for the gratuitous instruction of eight or ten children in addition to the number provided for by the endowment, and that by such arrangement more children derive benefit from the charity than the master would by the terms of the will be compellable to teach; it is also represented, and the fact is not doubted, that the children are very well instructed, and, would not be better instructed if the master personally attended at the school. From the inquiry we have made upon this subject, we are induced to conclude, under all the circumstances, that though the neglect of duty on the part of the master is not sufficiently excused, the advantage which might arise to the parish or the poorer inhabitants of Cottingham from the adoption of means of removing him, in compelling him to teach the scholars in person, is not sufficient in point either of importance or certainty to require from us the recommendation of legal proceedings for such purpose.[4]

Since 1785 when the money given by N. C. Burton, Esq. had been appropriated to enlarging the workhouse there had been no satisfactory accommodation for the schoolmaster. This problem was overcome in 1815 when a house now known as 'Church View' was built next to the school. This did not help to smooth the passage for the school however as more dissention arose in the 1830's after the death of Reverend Deans. It appears that in fact two schools were being taught – one by W. H. Carr, an assistant overseer of the poor and appointed Master of the Free School by the Parish, and the other by a person unknown teaching in a room above the workhouse adjacent to the school. Mr. Carr objected, not unnaturally; he also objected to the proposal to build a Church School and affiliate it to the National Schools. He thought, quite correctly as it turned out, that his pupils might be transferred to the new school and he lose his job. His protests had no effect on the building of the new school; they only served to highlight the dissentions over the Free School. It is not surprising that the Church proposed to build the new school in view of the turbulent career of the Free School especially when there was litigation between the parishioners and the Lord of the Manor regarding the

4 *Reports on Charities, York and East Riding*, p.743.

premises; arguments about appointments and dismissals of pupils at the school; and charges of embezzlement! And so when the new National School opened its doors, the thirty children of the Free School nominated by the Trustees attended there. This must have been a temporary arrangement as the Free School and its endowment existed again in 1846.

In 1857 Joseph Brittain was appointed Master of the Free School. He rented it at four shillings per year, paid quarterly agreeing to maintain the building in good repair. The agreement was subject to six months notice either way.

Brittain was eventually given notice to quit. He appealed to law. The Charity Commissioners stepped in and urged an early settlement to the dispute. Brittain agreed to go on payment of damages as he maintained that he had been given notice contrary to the agreement.

In November, 1876 Brittain said that he was teaching twenty boys gratis. There is no indication as to other monies involved. He was awarded damages but had to surrender the tenancy bringing to an end at last the very mixed career of the school. The endowments

Doorway of the Mark Kirby School, built in 1850.

26

were then applied to thirty poor children attending the Newland National School, the Cottingham National School and the Cottingham Wesleyan School. In 1894 the trustees resolved that changes should be made in the distribution of the charity.

'That the Funds be applied to assisting the education of poor children, by giving prizes to children of school age; by giving sums of money to children who have reached the age and standard of exemption and are willing to continue attending school; by establishing Exhibitions for children to continue their education at such places of Higher and Technical Education or for maintainence during apprenticeship at some useful trade.'[5]

Up to the abolition of school uniforms, the eight trustees administered the Charity toward helping with the cost of new uniforms for children attending Cottingham High School whose parents found difficulty in meeting the full payments.

The Mark Kirby School now occupying the site is not the original school. Late in the 17th century John Wardell established a dwelling to the south of St. Mary's Church known as 'Tothill Cottage' for twelve poor widows. It is possible that one or more of these ladies kept a school for poor local children for a few pence, giving Wardell the idea of a Free or Endowed School. According to the East Riding Registry of Deeds, a school in Cottingham Church Yard was in existence when Mark Kirby took over and endowed it in 1712, but it is impossible to ascertain the extent of the site. In 1729 Richard Burton Gent gave land in the vicinity of the school to 'the use of the Poor of Cottingham forever'. This building now known as Church House was bigger than at present and became the parish workhouse. The original schoolroom was not in existence when the National School was built, the children being taught in the workhouse by the workhouse master. When the workhouse inmates were transferred to Sculcoates in 1840 or 1841 the workhouse building was advertised to let. In 1850 the western end was demolished and a vestry room 'Arlington Hall' was built. In the same year a schoolroom was created separately at the eastern end. This may have been on the site of the original one, but this cannot be proved. It is certain that there is a gap in time somewhere between 1729 and 1850 when there was no school building functioning for the instruction of children only.

5   Mark Kirby Charity Minute Book.

This block of property is easily identifiable, approached along a causeway beside the church, the vestry room 'Arlington Hall'; the main body of the old workhouse now named Church House; the school bearing the painted inscription 'Mark Kirby Free School'; and detached but close by 'Church View' erected in 1815 for the master of the Mark Kirby Free School.

THE NATIONAL SCHOOL

The building which for years was known to Cottingham residents as the King Street Rooms, was erected in 1835 at a cost of about £200 and was opened on 11th January, 1836 as a National School. The need for further educational facilities in the village was stated to have been prompted by the grant of £20,000 made by the government in 1833 to be allocated to the voluntary religious societies for the provision of schools, the Anglican 'National Society' and the Non-conformist 'British and Foreign School Society.' The then Vicar of the Parish, the Rev. R. Barker supported by other interested people, decided to take advantage of the Act and succeeded in securing grants from H.M. Treasury of £100; the National Society £20; and the balance of the money was raised by voluntary contributions and local efforts such as bazaars.

At first a local committee was elected to carry through the project, then a Committee of Management took over and trustees were appointed. The names of the original men associated with the committee are known. The Vicar and Churchwardens were ex-officio members of the Committee of Management. There does not appear to be any subsequent record of new appointments to the Trustees, though this must have taken place.

The St. Mary's Church Council has in its possession a Declaration of Trust dated 2nd March, 1836 and enrolled in the High Court of Chancery 17th March, 1836, showing that the Cottingham National School was united to the National Society 'for promoting the education of the poor in the principles of the Established Church and to be conducted in conformity with the principles of that institution and towards the advancement of its ends and designs.' In the concluding sentences of the Declaration of Trust it is stated that if within three years there was no support for the Cottingham National School and no pupils were taught there, the trustees were to dispose of the property and after payments of any debts had to pay whatever surplus money there was to the National Society; or to the Treasury if the National Society was no longer in operation.

The building consisted of one long room initially, with a raised dais at one end for the Head. This was the pattern of the National Schools and indeed of the old grammar schools. Desks or tables were ranged around the walls for writing and reading, the children sitting on forms. The centre floor space was occupied by other pupils standing in groups and receiving instruction from monitors who helped the master or mistress with the instruction of the younger children. A similar pattern was in use in the British and Foreign schools, except that in those schools the centre floor space was occupied by the desks and forms, while the wall side areas were used for monitorial instruction. Monitors were pupils of ten or eleven years old who were personally instructed by the master or mistress and who then taught the younger pupils. The curriculum consisted of reading, writing and arithmetic in the early days of the National School, with geography, natural history and poetry being added in later years. The age for admission was six years and upwards and, except for the thirty free scholars from the Mark

King Street Rooms, Cottingham – the old National School shortly before its demolition.

The Headmaster, Mr. A. B. Moorby, with a group of boys at the National School building.

Kirby School, the fees were twopence a week for instruction in reading, writing on slates and the first four rules of arithmetic – with one penny for each additional child from the same family.

For fourpence a week an exercise book was provided for the written work, with twopence a week for additional children from the same family. Other books and slates were provided free. The Bible and various religious texts formed the staple diet of reading material. The books in the school were selected from the catalogue of the SPCK (Society for the Propagation of Christian Knowledge). The girls were to be employed for half of each day in needlework and knitting to prepare them for their expected future role in life as wives and mothers. The hours of schooling were from 9.00 a.m. to 12 noon and from 1.30 p.m. to 4.30 p.m.

Saturdays were holidays; other holidays were Shrove Tuesday afternoon; Good Friday to Easter Tuesday; Holy Thursday; Whit Monday and Tuesday; the King's birthday and anniversary of accession; the 5th of November and 29th of May; four weeks during harvest; and one week after Christmas Day.

In the return of Church Schools compiled by the National Society in 1846-47 the numbers attending were seventy-nine pupils, with a Master and Mistress at a joint salary of £70 per annum. The total expenditure was £85 and this seems to have been covered by subscriptions and the children's pence. There was an endowment for the children transferred from the Mark Kirby School shortly after the National School was built, numbering eleven at this time, and the value of that endowment at the time had increased to £40.

The 'monitorial' system of teaching was a very rigid one, It had its beginnings in India and was often referred to as the 'Madras' system. Dr. Andrew Bell used it in his military orphanage in Madras and as Superintendent personally taught some of the older and brighter pupils; they then instructed the rest of the pupils while Dr. Bell filled the role of Headmaster. When the National Society was formed in 1811, Dr. Bell became Superintendent of the Society's Central School in Baldwin Gardens, London for the training of schoolteachers, and the system was adopted there and in the various Diocesan training schools.

It was a system born of expediency – and it was economical. It was the answer to an increasing population demanding education for its young, and it was a means of instructing the maximum number of children as cheaply as possible to fit them for work in expanding industry and commerce.

In 1852 annual government grants began; there were 127 pupils attending at the school at the time. John Steel and Mary Ann Matthews were responsible for the teaching at a joint annual salary of £70. With a staff of two teachers being responsible for 127 pupils, we can see the need for monitorial help. The building was enlarged in 1859 to accommodate more infants. During the 1860's the average attendance was 259 pupils in summer and 376 in winter. This disparity is indicative of the fact that the bulk of Cottingham's population worked on the land or was largely connected with it and shows the importance of children's labour at hay-making, harvesting and other busy times of the agricultural year. There was no compulsory education until 1880 and even then it was not easy to persuade parents that it was their duty and responsibility to send their children to school regularly.

From about the middle of the last century and especially during the 1860's, the denominational schools found it increasingly difficult to keep pace with the growing demand for school places – demand exceeded supply and the religious bodies began to find that providing or extending schools was a heavy financial burden to shoulder. The Education Act of 1870 allowed the setting up of locally elected School Boards whose task it was to assess the existing provision of schools in their area and, if necessary, build new ones. They could also, after agreement with the local denominational school trustees, take over the management and day to day running of their schools, with powers to levy rates and where necessary to provide extra accommodation for the children. Early in 1877 both the National and Wesleyan schools in Cottingham came to arrangements with the local School Board.

The Board met at the Vestry Rooms (now named Arlington Hall), in March, 1877 – the members of the Board will be referred to more fully later. Plans of the existing schools were produced and discussed and a census of all children in the area was authorised. At its monthly meeting in April the Board decided that the accommodation in the National School building was proving inadequate. It was a mixed school as was the Wesleyan School in Northgate and some relief of the pressure of numbers was evidently going to be secured by keeping all the boys at the National School,

A teacher and pupils at the 'old school' building, King Street Rooms

sending the girls to the Wesleyan School and concentrating the infants at the Primitive Methodists Sunday School building in King Street (north); an Area Health Authority is housed now on the site. Similarly, the Wesleyan School would send all its boys to the National building and keep its girls in Northgate. At the May meeting, the Board authorised the advertisement of its Notice of Occupation of both buildings. The Board also took over the management of the Newland National School in August. 1877 was a very busy year for the newly formed Cottingham School Board. In the same year a young man named A. B. Moorby was appointed as a pupil teacher in the Newland National School; he was destined to play an important part in the education of Cottingham children. T. Jameson was Headmaster of Cottingham National School in 1877.

Things were evidently put on a firmer basis when a Memorandum of Arrangement was drawn up on the 15th March, 1883, between Edward Foster Coulson, the sole surviving member of the Cottingham National School Committee of Trustees, and the School Board of Cottingham, when it was agreed that the Board

Pupils and their teacher at the King Street Schoolroom.

should have the exclusive use of the school and pay all rates, taxes, insurances, etc. in connection with the building for the next four years. They were to keep the building clean and in good and tenantable repair internally and externally. This arrangement had the consent of the subscribers to the National School.

Mr. T. Jameson, who had been appointed Head in May, 1877, resigned and was awarded a pension. His place was taken by Mr. A. B. Moorby, the former pupil teacher at Newland School, at an annual salary of £100, in June, 1885. In January of the following year his wife, Mrs. Annie Moorby was appointed Headmistress of the infants' school at an annual salary of £50.

The following salaries were paid to the staff of the Board's Schools in March, 1891 – salaries were paid quarterly:

At the boys' school:

A. B. Moorby. Master	£25	0	0
An assist. Master	£14	0	0
An assist. Mistress	£7	10	0
A pupil teacher	£6	10	0
Monitors	£1	6	0

At the girls' school:

M. Ellerker. Mistress	£22	10	0
Assist. Mistress	£10	0	0
Pupil teachers	£11	12	6
Monitors	£1	6	0

At the infants' school:

A. Moorby. Mistress	£18	10	0
A pupil teacher	£7	15	0

Mrs. Moorby's salary had been fixed at £74 per annum at the infants' school in November, 1890. The children's fees remained virtually the same as they were when the school began in 1836 – two pence a week in the infants' school, three pence a week in the boys' and the girls' schools or two pence each for three or more pupils from the same family.

Mr. Moorby was Headmaster of the boys' school in Cottingham from 1885 until his death in 1923. He was one of the most respected and popular men in the village along with the Rector and the local policeman. Recreational space was very limited at the old National School, so the boys played football or cricket on Market Green at break or lunch time and Mr. Moorby often joined in, running around as enthusiastically as any of his boys. He was a disciplinarian, but a fair one. As one old pupil recalled, 'he was a grand chap – mind you he gave you "what for" if you deserved it, but lads never bore a grudge against him – he treated you as you deserved one way or t'other.' A fitting epitaph to a well loved Headmaster.

According to Mr. H. R. Wright, a member of the Church Council and a Governor of Hallgate School, the St. Mary's Church records show no payments by the Church to the National Society for the use of the building; from the time that the school was no longer held there the upkeep and maintainance was shouldered by the Church alone. The Parochial Church Council gained possession of the title deeds in 1967.

There does not appear to be the amount of detail available on the National School as regards the day to day running of the school, inspections, examinations, teachers helpers etc., as there does on the Wesleyan School. However, there must have been visits from Her Majesty's Inspectors of Schools (HMI's) as the allocation of the government grants from the early 1860's shared annually between the Voluntary Societies depended upon the efficient administration of the various schools, the attendance of the pupils and the success of the pupils in their annual examinations.

If the pupils were successful in their exams they passed on to the next Standard, hence the old terminology 'Standard' 1 or 2 or 3 and so on – the forerunner of Class or Form 1 or 2 or 3 etc. The Standard not only meant moving 'up' to the next class each year, but significantly, the Standard of work resulting from the year in that class. The annual exams built into the system in the 1860's were kept up by the School Boards as a measure of efficiency. So, as the National School in Cottingham was begun with help from the Treasury, it is assumed that grant aid was received regularly.

The building was put to a variety of uses when its time as a day school ended. St. Mary's Church used it for religious instruction, youth movements and jumble sales. Cottingham ladies opened a canteen for troops there during the last war, and it was used by the WRVS as a 'Darby and Joan' Club from about 1950 until the present Club was opened in Finkle Street in 1955. One of the last uses to which the rooms were put was as a weekly school of ballet and tap dancing, continuing its original association with

Cottingham's children.

The old school building is now gone. It has been replaced by the Elm Tree Court flats fronting King Street (south), and the two shops just inside Finkle Street. The old school building extended along King Street to about the vehicle entry to the flats and Post office; in fact almost alongside William Green's original school. It must have been a welcome step forward in the education of Cottingham's children, bringing as it did instruction within the reach of parents unable to afford the fees of the private schools. Its days as a school ended in 1893 when pupils and staff transferred to the newly erected Board School – the present Hallgate Junior School.

THE WESLEYAN SCHOOL

In 1870 the Education Act setting up School Boards received Royal Assent on the 9th August. There followed a tremendous spurt of activity on the part of many voluntary bodies to provide education for children of their religious denominations. The Wesleyan authorities in the Cottingham area are an excellent example of the speed with which a day school could be provided within one year, later cut to six months, by the terms of the Act. In 1869 the attendance at the Sunday School averaged 192 pupils and this must have influenced the decision to provide a day school. There had been a Sunday School in the village, certainly since 1858.

Work proceeded at a feverish pace and on the 9th January, 1871 the day school was opened adjacent to the Chapel then situated on the north side of Northgate nearly opposite the junction with King Street. The Wesleyan Methodist Chapel is no longer standing, the congregation having moved to the newly built Chapel in Hallgate in 1878. The Salvation Army building occupies the site now. Just as the National School was built practically next to William Green's original school, so the Wesleyan School was close by William's later school (the Northgate House site). The walled pathway giving access to the playing fields separates the two sites.

When the day school opened it admitted seventy scholars but by the 13th January there were 119 boys and 61 girls and by the 20th January, 138 boys and 113 girls, making a total of 251 pupils. Attendance came to vary a great deal because it was not then compulsory. The first master was Joseph Hughes and he reported in his daily entries in the school log book that pupils were absent because of bad weather or working in the fields or visiting Hull Fair; at one time one third of the pupils was absent because of measles. Holidays seem to have been frequent – religious anniversaries, feasts, and indicative again of the agricultural connections of the village, holidays for farm servants. The writer remembers the autumn half-term holiday in October being still referred to as 'potato picking' just after the last war.

Mr. Hughes had the assistance of a group of village ladies who came in on a rota basis to teach sewing to the girls. The basis of teaching was the three R's with of course, appropriate religious instruction. Departure from the usual curricula is indicated by lessons on 'The Elephant', 'The Fox' and 'The Bear'. Singing was also a feature, hymns and songs with a distinctly religious flavour. A. Payne was appointed pupil teacher on 1st December, 1871.

This was the period of 'Payment by Results'. Inspectors paid regular visits to the school to conduct the annual examinations upon the results of which rested the amount of grant received; proof of the State's willingness to promote good relationships with the voluntary schools is indicated by the local example of the Reverend G. French inspecting the school in its first year. Perhaps not unnaturally he reported favourably:

'Only a few children were presented but they passed a very satisfactory examination in elementary subjects. Mr. Hughes has begun well and his evident conscientiousness, energy and industry promise great success for the future. I was pleased with all that I saw and heard in this school. The singing is nice and the needlework pretty good.'[1]

The Government grant for the year was £31.8.4. As regards the examination results, these are as follows:

		Reading		Writing		Arithmetic	
		Boys	Girls	Boys	Girls	Boys	Girls
January	I	84.6	80.8	51.8	69.7	63.8	40.1
	II	90.3	81.7	88.3	86.5	55.6	48.1
February	I	87.6	81.5	69.2	54.2	60.8	35.8
	II	81.9	83.3	48.3	31.3	66.2	50.6
March	I	93.4	86.5	57.1	36.8	60.6	27.0
	II	88.8	84.6	68.3	73.8	44.8	44.0

The numbers of pupils fluctuated, around 60 average then up to 106 at the examination. As can be seen the boys achieved the better all-round results. The Reverend J. Tucker, the Superintendent Minister, was jubilant in his report on the operation of the school in its first year.

1   Report on Schools in Beverley Circuit – Schedule I Day Schools.

'beyond expectation. What is wanted there is additional school accommodation. If new premises could be obtained it would be a great boon to our cause in that important village'.[2]

In January, 1872, the trustees met and agreed to extend the school. Subscriptions and bazaars raised £420 and building began, again an indication of the race against the School Boards. The building was opened in January 1873. The first master, Mr. Hughes, had left and his successor Mr. H. Hutchinson reported:

'Everything is on a larger and better scale. Several ladies and gentlemen called to look over the rooms'.[3]

Mr. Hutchinson appears to have expanded the curriculum; mapping, drill, history, local geography, spelling, and climate were introduced. Mention is made very briefly to a pupil teacher – Norah Horsaman who began by being a monitor – and was taught by the next master personally from seven to eight each morning!

On 5th January, 1874 Mr. R. Fretwell took over as Master and made some changes in the routine of the school but does not record what the changes were. There must have been continued improvement in the pupils' abilities as eight of them received

A teacher – Miss Ellerker? – with a group of girls at the old Wesleyan School building.

2   Ibid.
3   Wesleyan School Log Book, p.27.

certificates of proficiency in handwriting, twenty-one achieving a high standard altogether. Yet the Her Majesty's Inspector's report for the master's first year was not too glowing:

> 'In Standard I arithmetic was weak and didn't know their tables . . . in paperwork, spelling was far from what it should be but handwriting is fair. Reading and arithmetic of infants should receive more attention and Primers and History cards should be provided for them. What sewing there was seemed poorly done; cutting out, darning and patching should be taught. The discipline is defective and must be kept under better control'.[4]

Mr. Fretwell evidently tightened up on discipline, keeping a boy in over the dinner hour because he was away without good reason and persuading another boy to do the same thing; a girl was punished for stealing another pupil's orange; two boys were punished for stealing; and two boys punished for fighting. The average attendance for the week ending March 6th, 1874 was 68.7% This would seem to be about the average for the remainder of the Wesleyan School's life.

On November 4th Mr. Fretwell received a form from the Science and Art Department and on March 5th, a Drawing Examination took place. Evidently the school was in receipt of occasional grants from the Science and Art Department.

The Inspector's report dated April 7th, 1875 is mixed:

> 'The attendance of the children at this school is very irregular and uncertain. Not one half of those present on the day of inspection could be put on the examination schedule. Mr. Fretwell is evidently a most conscientious and painstaking Master and under better circumstances would, I doubt not, do very well indeed. The elementary examination was on the whole pretty good. The spelling and arithmetic seem to be the weakest subjects. The general tone, order and discipline are very creditable. The singing is duly taught and the sewing satisfactory. N. Horsaman should improve in all subjects'.[5]

On August 14th, 1876 Mr. Fretwell wrote,

> 'called myself on some of the parents to impress on them the necessity of sending their children more regularly',[6]

4 Report on Schools in Beverley Circuit – Schedule I Day Schools.
5 Wesleyan School Log Book, p.36.
6 Ibid p.50.

And on November 25th, found,

> 'it is almost impossible to get through the work of the Code under present circumstances'.[7]

The Code was the regulations governing the payment of grant based on the pupils' attendance and exam results and the difficulties referred to by Mr. Fretwell were as a result of an outbreak of measles in the village; the attendance did not improve until nearly Christmas. On December 22nd a magic lantern show was given.

An ominous entry as far as the Wesleyan School was concerned appears on January 31st, 1877, when reference is made to a School Board Election in the village. On March 2nd an irate mother took her children away because they were kept in to learn their nine times table.

On March 5th the Inspector's Report said that,

> 'A very considerable improvement has taken place in the attainments of the older children and the infants are satisfactorily advanced except in Reading and Tables. Reading and Spelling is with the children examined in standards particularly creditable and neatness of Handwriting commendable. In arithmetic failures have resulted from inaccuracy. Answering in Grammar and Geography is satisfactory. The poetry taken for literature was too simple and only moderately well known.
>
> If a cupboard were provided for keeping needlework the girls might all show some specimen of their sewing. I saw no knitting, darning, patching, nor cutting out and only about half of the girls present showed any work'.[8]

On March 16th Mr. Fretwell applied for the Headship when the school was ultimately transferred to the Cottingham School Board. He was unsuccessful.

In June, 1877 the school was transferred to the Cottingham School Board. From then on it admitted girls only; the master left at the same time.

The new School Boards elected as a result of the 1870 Act were to have at least five and a maximum of fifteen members. Cottingham Board was composed of five well known local residents, David Wilson, Esq., Chairman; Reverend Thomas Rain, Congregational Minister, Vice-Chairman; Mr. Daniel

7   Ibid p.66.
8   Report on Schools in Beverley Circuit – Schedule I Day Schools.

Stonehouse, a Wesleyan lay preacher; Mr. G. Tranmer, a pork butcher and trustee of the Primitive Methodist Chapel; and Mr. W. J. Atkinson. Clearly, the cause of non-conformity was not going to suffer thereby and the compromises established by the State and the Churches were thus secured in Cottingham at any rate.

At the national level Her Majesty's Inspectors frequently complained of the social composition of the School Boards and lack of experience and knowledge of education. It should be realised that many of the trustees of the former non-conformist schools had no experience or knowledge of education either. Many were tradespeople, farmers, even labourers, but they all had the interests of the children at heart; they were trustees of the spiritual, moral and educational well-being of their particular flock. Dissention would occur – it occurs in more academic circles than those. The trustees were therefore well known and highly respected, and usually respectable citizens. The School Boards were in many cases an extension of the same situation, but merging or submerging the sectional interests of all members.

The School Board paid the Wesleyan Trustees £32.4.6 for the

A view of Northgate about 1900; the old Wesleyan Chapel and School can just be seen at the far left of the picture.

school equipment. A schoolmistress was engaged to teach the girls, a Miss M. E. Crosby at a salary of £70 per year. The fee for the school was 3d. a week; 2d. if the pupil was from a large family. In January, 1878 pupils were provided with school books. Miss Crosby had three pupil teachers and a monitor to help her; the pupil teachers' salaries varied from between £8 and £14 per year according to age and experience. An attendance officer was authorised to take proceedings against parents who did not send their children to the Board School; this was as yet a by-law until the 1880 Act made school attendance obligatory.

In April, 1887 Miss Margaret Ellerker was appointed Headmistress of the Girls' Board School at an annual salary of £75.

The school rooms were used by the Board until 3rd July, 1893 as the girls' department. The arrangement was proving unsatisfactory; the population had grown from 4,015 in 1871 to 6,177 in 1881 and to 10,103 in 1891 with a proportionate increase in the necessity for more school places. Consequently section 18 from Part 1 of the Education Act of 1870 was invoked:

'The School Board shall from time to time provide such additional school accommodation as is in their opinion necessary in order to supply a sufficient amount of public school accommodation for their district'.[9]

A site was acquired adjacent and to the north of St. Mary's Church in Hallgate and building commenced along the now familiar Board School architectural lines which were to become a feature of English cities, towns and villages at the end of the last century. The school was built at a cost of £8,048. School fees were to be 2d. a week for infants, 3d. for the rest, or 2d. if there were more than three in the family. A monitor was appointed for the infants at 2/- per week. Accommodation was for 800 boys, girls and infants.

9 *The Education Act of 1870*, J. Murphy, p.41. (1971).

THE SCHOOL BOARD ERA:
GIRLS' SCHOOL HALLGATE

When the children of the old National and Wesleyan Schools arrived at their new abode on Monday the 3rd of July, 1893, they found a vastly different building awaiting them. Large light classrooms replaced their old quarters; boys and girls continued to be segregated though the infants were kept together, a situation which was to persist until 1968 or 69 when boys and girls were brought together again in the same classrooms. To a casual observer the old Hallgate School building would probably appear to be all of the same age, but in fact the group of buildings in the centre of the blocks closest to the foothpath and those to the east were the original School Board buildings, as the legend above the window overlooking the footpath testifies – 'Cottingham Board School 1892'. The centre and east blocks are interconnected, the infants were housed in the centre from the beginning and the older children in the east block. The building standing well back from the footpath to the west of these buildings was added in 1911 because of pressure of numbers and became the boys' department, the older east wing becoming the girls' department until the 1960's.

The layout of the original building has changed little over the years. The majority of the infants were taught in the hall overlooking the footpath. Nowadays we tend to think of a school hall being used for assembly, concerts, PE, parents' meetings, even as a dining area for pupils staying for school lunches. But originally these halls were just large classrooms accommodating several classes, or standards, of children with the addition of several smaller rooms to cater for extra pupils. The 'big room' was often divided by folding doors or screens which could be opened out to convert it into an assembly or PE area.

So it was at Cottingham Board School. Mrs. Jones of Southwood Farm remembers that there was a gallery at the back of the infants' hall with steps leading up to it in a corner; some children were taught in this gallery. The Headmistress of the infants, Mrs. Moorby, had her office off the infants' 'big room'. The admissions, or 'babies', were housed in the first classroom through the hall, leaving three classrooms along that corridor occupied by girls. Their Headmistress's room was at the end of this corridor with their 'big room' on the right. Standards one to three used the classrooms, standards four to seven being taught in the 'big room'.

The boys occupied the eight remaining classrooms at the end of the block. There were in effect three schools as formerly but housed now on the same site. Boys, girls and infants each had their own playground. The boys had a maypole in theirs – this caused some jealousy amongst the girls. There were some swings however in the girls' playground. The boys' playground was through the gates on the right, or east, of the infants' hall with the entrance to their school at the bottom of the playground. The entrance to the infant section was through the large wooden door facing the footpath, with their playground on the left, or west side. The entrance to the girls' department was through the door on the same side, at the end of the infants' hall but facing their playground. The

The exterior of the Infants' Hall, or 'big room', showing the elaborate work around the inscription above the windows.

46

girls' playground was beyond. All toilets were outside.

The construction of the school wall at the eastern end was the cause of complaints from the occupier of a cottage close by. He said that the high brick wall excluded light from his back garden. The difficulty was overcome when the School Board offered him compensation of £25 on the 9th of June, 1892!

The girls actively helped in the move from the old school to the new one; potted plants and boxes of sewing were carried round to the Hallgate premises. Most of the heavy items, including books and slates, were packed away several days earlier ready for the carrier's cart – much to the delight of the pupils! Miss Ellerker transferred along with her girls and continued in her capacity as Headmistress of the girls' school, later marrying and becoming Mrs. Holmes.

The Wesleyan School Log Book was continued as the Girls' School Log Book when the School Board took over the Northgate School, and subsequently in the new building in Hallgate. The first entry in the new school reads:

> 'Commenced duties on Monday morning in the new schools which are situated in Hallgate. The Chairman (of the School Board) Mr. Stonehouse visited this department on Monday morning. A holiday was granted to the children on Wednesday on account of the Cottingham Club Feast and on Thursday in honour of the Royal Wedding. On Friday there was a very poor attendance'.[1]

The Cottingham Club Feast was held annually. In those days before the Welfare State there were many small assurance groups in operation; Cottingham United Friendly Society was one of them. Working men who could afford to do so subscribed a few pence each week to their chosen club. In times of sickness or death the club provided a small income in return for these contributions. The Feast was a procession and a dinner for the members, with a round-about on Market Green and numerous stalls which overflowed into King Street; the gentlemen usually adjourned to a local hostelry! The fair that visits Market Green each year is the survivor of the Cottingham Club Feast.

The Royal Wedding referred to was that of the future George V and Princess Mary of Teck on the 6th of July, 1893. No wonder there was a poor attendance at school on the Friday after two

1   Wesleyan School Log Book, p.231.

successive days of jollification in the village! The few children that attended that day did so to the usual ringing of the bell above the infants' hall, or 'big room', by a big lad from the boys' department at 8.55 a.m., after which Mrs. Holmes appeared ringing a hand bell at 9 a.m. sharp. According to Mrs. Jones, this was the routine each school day morning.

Family circumstances were sharply contrasted. In February 1893 two girls had left the school in Northgate in order to attend the Hull Higher Grade School – the present Brunswick Junior High School, just off Beverley road, Hull. As the title indicates, more advanced work was taught there to older pupils and a place cost 9d. per week, although in some cases scholarships were awarded. Two other girls left, one aged eleven and the other twelve, to take up positions as domestic servants; at about the same time two more left to go into the Union Workhouse because of poverty at home. The minimum school leaving age was fixed at eleven years in 1893 and was raised to twelve years in 1899.

The average attendance in August, 1893 was 124 girls and a grant of nineteen shillings per child was earned. The total grant was

The old entrance to the Infants' Department

£119.16.0. Singing and English were recommended as subjects which in future were to earn a higher grant from the Education Department. Poor attendance appears to have been a problem well into the School Board era. References are constantly made in the Log Book to lists of names being reported to the Board for the attention of the Attendance Officer.

Outbreaks of measles, whooping cough and scarlet fever were common and reference is made on one occasion to an outbreak of diphtheria in the village. No doubt the majority of absences were due to children having to work in the fields and gardens of the area. Bad weather is also given as a cause of absence; children living a long way off having difficulty getting to school in snow or through muddy tracks. The girls were often kept at home to look after younger brothers or sisters if the mother was ill or helping on the land at busy times. Indeed, girls sometimes left school altogether at ten years old to look after younger members of the family. Consequently there were fewer children in the classes toward the top of the school; children could leave school at ten years provided that they had put in a certain total number of attendances – this was known as the 'Dunces Pass'. This situation ended when the school leaving age was set at a minimum of eleven years old, although School Boards could compel attendance up to the age of thirteen – corresponding to Standard VII. Several older Cottingham ex-pupils vouch for the fact that at times there were only four or five girls in Standard VII, the rest having left school with the permission of the Board.

At the end of September, 1893, permission was granted for the Mistress to attend a cookery class organised by the County Council in Cottingham. This was held somewhere in Northgate according to a reference in the Archives Office in Beverley. From this is inferred a further extension of the curriculum.

The various Standards were examined by members of the Board each week with regularity. The then Rector of St. Mary's, the Reverend H. P. Ramsden, particularly interested himself in the progress of the pupils as did the Chairman of the Board, Mr. Stonehouse. The pupil teachers were taught by the staff either at 8.00 a.m. or after the school closed in the afternoon. In April, 1894, they were allowed to study for their examinations during lesson times prior to the examination day. In the same month Standard III began to do their work on paper instead of on slates.

In February, 1899 figures of the teachers' salaries appear. Assistants received from £40 to £45 per annum. After passing the 1st year's certificate examination papers the salary was £50 per annum and a certificated assistant received £60 per year. The average attendance of the pupils was 165 and they received a grant of £1 per head. At the end of August a staff of nine is recorded including three pupil teachers, a monitor and a Senior Mistress; seven standards were taught. A crisis occurred at this time as two of the staff left the school and in spite of efforts by the Board no replacements were found until after the Christmas holidays when a lady who had formerly been a pupil teacher at the Day Street British School was appointed to Hallgate girls' department.

The HMI's report for that year commented that much favourable work had been done in spite of staff difficulties and recommended the higher grants for class subjects once again. The Mistress asked the Board's permission to keep back for another year several scholars who were not eligible to be promoted to a higher standard.

In February, 1900 bad weather and measles struck the village.

Inside the Infants' Hall – showing original buttress work and windows.

A series of snow storms cut attendances down to 86 out of 171. Between February 20th and March 19th the whole school was closed due to a severe outbreak of measles. On Monday, May 20th the whole school was given a day's holiday to celebrate the relief of Mafeking!

Further evidence of the need for child labour in the predominantly agricultural area is given in June, 1900 when an agitated HMI was told that only 159 children out of a total of 206 in the girls' school were present – one quarter were absent working on the land especially from the upper standards. Holidays were given for a variety of reasons – two days for Hull Fair; one day for Cottingham Club Feast; a day for the Wesleyan Feast; a day for the Methodists' picnic; a day for the Queen's Birthday, and so on, showing a largely insular and rural life. There are many references, often to long lists of children being reported to the monthly meetings of the School Board for poor attendances and of the Board taking up the matter with the parents, often to little effect apparently, but in November, 1900 the Board decided to prosecute one parent, perhaps as an example as his child had had many

The old entrance to the Girls' Department.

Mrs. Moorby on the left and an assistant teacher with some of the infants – location unknown.

absences.

The average attendance for the school year ending August, 1901 was 174 and the grant consisted of twenty-one shillings per scholar. The total grant received was £182.14.0. A staff of eight is recorded including the Senior Mistress.

In December, 1901 the Chairman of the School Board, Mr. D. Stonehouse, who had been a member since the first days of the School Board in 1877, died. In the same month the Reverend H. P. Ramsden died, also. Both men had devoted many years toward the well-being of Cottingham's children in the last decades of the nineteenth century and a good response was received for subscriptions for wreaths for the two funerals of men divided in religion but united in education.

One June 2nd and 3rd, 1902 a holiday was given to celebrate the declaration of Peace after the Boer War. In October of the same year a week's holiday was authorised by the Board to celebrate the coronation of King Edward VII. The Schools were closed because of an outbreak of measles between February 24th and March 16th, 1903.

The following entry in the Log Book is a brief but ominous one as far as the Board was concerned:

'Week Ending April 10th, 1903. The Board held their final meeting on Monday evening as the East Riding County Council are taking the Management of the Schools'.[2]

Yet despite the changeover brought about by the Education Act of 1902 creating Local Education Authorities, there was no dramatic upheaval at the school. Things progressed much the same up to the final entries in the Log Book in 1904 with the possible exception of the decline in the number of arbitrary holidays which used to be awarded by the Board. Various gentlemen visited the school, some of them old Board members and the local Anglican and Non-conformist clergy continued to display their respective interests in the school. But the 'wind of change' was evidently blowing through the whole school by August 13th, 1903, the date of the HMI's report:

'Order and neatness called for specially favourable notice and class changes are quietly and smartly effected. Strenuous efforts have been made to impart the instruction on broader and more educational lines, to awaken more interest on the part of the girls, to give more variety to the routine and generally to bring the methods into conformity with the spirit of the current Code. Further advance is yet necessary and the teaching of composition in particular can be made more useful. Reading is creditable throughout. Spelling needs care, paper exercises are receiving increased attention and with encouraging results. The class teachers are evidently anxious to do their best in fulfilling their respective duties'.[3]

2   Wesleyan School Log Book, p.323.
3   Ibid. 353.

Mrs. Holmes, Headmistress of the Girls' department, with a class, or standard, of girls.

Teacher and girls taken at the newly opened Hallgate Schools, about 1895.

THE SCHOOL BOARD ERA:
BOYS' SCHOOL, HALLGATE

The first entry in the Boys' School Log Book is dated Monday, 3rd of July, 1893 and reads as follows:

> 'Opened in the new schools with a good muster of scholars. Mr. Stonehouse (Chairman of the School Board) was present for twenty minutes. The boys are delighted with the lightness of the rooms compared with the old school. Attention to lessons suffered by reason of the strangeness of the surroundings'.[1]

On Monday, 21st of August, 1893 there were a total of 220 boys on the registers – there were eight classrooms so the average number of boys per room at that time was just over 27. The total number of boys on the registers remained fairly static during the decade 1893-1903, whereas the numbers in the girls' department increased steadily during the decade. Mr. A. B. Moorby transferred as Headmaster with his boys from the old National School building, with a staff of six teachers. The records show a shortage of staff, even the Head having to cope with three separate standards on his own at times during the following weeks as some members of staff left to go to other schools. The first HMI's report for the Boys' School is a satisfactory one although it is stated that discipline could be tightened up.

Irregular attendance plagued the school as it did the girls' department. There are frequent references to lists of boys' names being sent to Mr. Jameson, the Board's Attendance Officer. In September the Head punished two boys for constantly playing truant. A parent removed his two boys from the school to the choir and school of Holy Trinity Church, Hull, expressing his satisfaction at the way his boys had been treated whilst at the school.

1 Boys' School Log Book, 1878-1899, p.329.

In October, the shortage of staff was still a problem, one class being sent to join a class in the girls' section; this was alleviated by an ex-pupil teacher from the girls' section joining the staff in the boys' section and taking Standard I. Monitors were used to supplement staff shortages as quickly as possible. The Head was obviously a Gilbert and Sullivan enthusiast as he records teaching songs from *Iolanthe* and others of their works to the boys; evidently the singing lessons were generally satisfactory.

All Standards were regularly examined as in the girls' department. Enterprising classes were rewarded for work over and above the usual routine work. For example, Standards VI and VII had gathered specimens of leaves, had identified them then pressed and mounted them, much to the delight of the Head, who rewarded the best efforts with a prize. Prize giving was a feature of the school year, usually taking place prior to the Christmas holidays. Parents attended, as did all the members of the School Board and the clergy of the village; the Chairman of the Board presented the prizes, usually books, to the pupils.

Thrift was encouraged in the school. Pennies were taken to

Staff photo – probably the earliest photograph of the combined staffs of the new schools in Hallgate. On the front row are Mrs. Moorby on the left, Mr. Moorby in the centre, Mrs. Holmes on the right, with three pupil teachers.

Mr. Moorby and one of the classes, about 1900.

school on Monday mornings by those able to afford to do so. A reference appears on Monday, 4th of June, 1894, to a Mr. Thackeray of Yorkshire Penny Bank going to the school and making a routine examination of the School Bank Books.

On Thursday, 7th of June the Standard VII boys had a practice examination in view of the County Scholarship examination at Beverley on the 16th of June, for entry to the Grammar School there. On Wednesday the 13th a half-day holiday was declared as only fifty per cent of the children attended in the morning. The Wesleyan Sunday School Feast was given as the cause! Eighteen boys were absent 'pulling ketlocks'. Ketlocks are a tall growing tough weed often appearing in corn crops. This again emphasises the predominantly agricultural environment of the area. A further extension of the activities of the school appears in July, 1894:

> 'The museum of specimens was opened today and is a great attraction to the boys who have responded well in presenting contributions'.[2]

This was a series of glass cases containing fossils, butterflies and so

2 Cottingham Boys' School Log Book 1878-1899, p.353.

on ranged against a corridor wall.

Three boys were successful in the County Examination for Beverley Grammar School that year. Higher grants were earned for the class subjects, English, History and Geography in the year. The use of monitors is criticised by the Head several times. For example:

'Examination of Standard II shows that it is almost impossible for a young raw monitor to have complete control of a class and make anything like headway with work. Both arithmetic and spelling are very weak and feeble and in some respects they have gone back'.[3]

The attendance got so bad at one stage that a lower grant was earned much to the anger of the Head who immediately initiated a scheme whereby a ticket was given to each boy to pin to his clothes bearing the words 'Never absent – never late'. Punctuality and attendance improved – at least for a time until the novelty wore off. At the end of August, 1895 the grant was at the rate of 18/6 per head plus £3.16.8 for specific subjects plus £6 for Pupil Teacher

3   Cottingham Boys' School Log Book, 1878-1899, p.370.

A pupil teacher with his class, or standard.

58

Grants. The average attendance for the year was 169 boys. There were 219 on the books.

In March, 1896 the whole school was closed because of an epidemic of measles and mumps. Including the Easter holidays, the school was shut for one month.

In 1897 it is recorded that there were seven Standards and ex-Standard VII and only six teachers all told including the Head. He and the assistant master were certificated; the rest were pupil teachers or ex-pupil teachers hoping to pass their qualifying examinations. The deficiencies were made up by a succession of unsatisfactory monitors causing the comments previously outlined. The Board agreed to pay the teachers' salaries monthly instead of quarterly.

There are repeated references to the lack of warmth in the school despite the efforts of the caretaker. During the worst of the winter months the thermometer never reached 52°F all morning. The pipes were never hot and in some rooms were quite cold although the boiler was at a 'fierce heat'. An engineer was called in to advise.

In July, 1898 there were 225 boys on the books and 184 in attendance showing that illness, truancy and land work took a big toll on education in the boys' department as it did in the girls. The Head records that the staff were under a great strain especially as the only other certificated teacher left to be Head of Dunswell School. No replacement was found for some months despite advertising by the Board and the Head was teaching two standards himself. In the same month two boys passed the County Scholarship Examination for Beverley Grammar School and applied for and received grants to help with clothing and so on from Mark Kirby's Charity.

Although slates were still being used in 1899 – boys hit each other with them – the harmonium was replaced by a piano, much improving the quality of the singing lessons and of drill. Paper was gradually replacing the use of slates however at this time from the top standards extending downwards.

On Wednesday, 24th May, 1899 a day's holiday was given in honour of Queen Victoria's eightieth birthday. In the same month a school library was started, the books being donated by the Head, the teachers and the pupils, as the Board said that since there were library facilities at the various Sunday Schools, they did not propose to provide one in the school.

From July, 1900 the curriculum was rapidly extended, Algebra was proposed as a special subject for grant but was disallowed although it continued to be taught. Botany was firmly introduced, also 'agricultural botany' with lessons on soils, drainage, manures, etc., very useful for the boys whose descendants are still farming or market gardening in the Cottingham area. Even lessons on the right way to till the soil were given to Standard VII. It is recorded that most boys had a fair practical knowledge of the subject – ploughs, scrufflers, harrows and rollers were all familiar to them.

The heating of the school had not improved by November, 1900 and seven gas heaters were installed to boost the warmth. In December the school was thoroughly cleaned and painted and the classroom walls colour washed during the holidays. New pictures, maps and so on were put up and the whole school took on a fresh invigorating look which was reflected in the new impetus to work of most of the boys. They evidently responded to lessons on 'Vascular and Cellular Tissues' and the 'Planetary System', with great interest. Field walks were initiated to the delight of the pupils. In April, 1901 the Board ruled that boys who were over 13 years old

A teacher and his boys.

60

could leave the school.

By August, 1901 a succession of reports records a full staff. This situation perhaps reacted upon the new enthusiasm which can be detected to be prevalent in the school at this time, teachers and pupils working together on new and often exciting interests. Truancy declined and the overall attendance improved gradually. The HMI's report of July, 1902 said:

'This is a very efficiently managed school and the results are eminently satisfactory. The staff are indefatigable in their efforts to improve the work'.[4]

Not a little credit for the above reference must go to the Headmaster himself. Mr. A. Barker of Kirby Drive, Cottingham, started in the infants' department before the turn of the century, and attended the boys' school. He describes Mr. and Mrs. Moorby as kindly, caring disciplinarians, devoted to the children in their charge.

4   Cottingham Boys' School Log Book, 1899-1902, p.72.

The exterior of the original Boys' Department.

CONCLUSION

It is sad to reflect that the names of many boys appearing in the Hallgate Boys' School Log Book also appear on the 1914-1918 war memorials in St. Mary's Church Yard and at the gates of the Memorial Gardens in Hallgate, Cottingham. Over 100 old boys of Cottingham's schools were killed in the First World War.

In St. Mary's Church is a memorial to three Cottingham sisters, the Misses Frances, Elizabeth and Mary Travis. These ladies were dedicated to working for the poor of Cottingham during the last century. Between them they founded and taught a Sunday School in the parish which was established in 1816. They all lived to a great age; one of them died in 1876 aged 100 years and four weeks.

It is possible that a school was held in St. Mary's long before the 19th century. There was a priest's room over the south porch up to the last century that was dismantled because it was thought unsafe. Stone benches exist now in the porch with faded traces of an inscription above them in the sandstone walls.

The Wesleyan School had a precedent. In Archbishop Herring's Visitation Returns of 1743 are recorded 277 families in the parish, one family per house. Of these 277 families, 122 were 'Dissenters' totalling some 300 people of all ages. These met twice on Sundays in a Licensed meeting house, according to their 'teacher'. This could indicate a Sunday School going back perhaps beyond that of the Misses Travis.

The private schools were a transitory affair. Many of them appear in the *Hull Advertiser* for only a year or two; some even less, then they disappear according to the fortunes of the master or mistress who operated them. Most of them were small and must have varied in efficiency. The advertisements for all of them were rather pretentious, but one can glimpse the differences between the several types. There are those which advertised regularly, over a period of several years; Green's seminary existed for forty years offering a broad curriculum to those parents willing to pay for the instruction of their children. Then there are those schools which appear only once or twice. This could indicate a lack of success but was not necessarily so as the school might have had a good reputation which needed no advertising. There were others operated by women catering for a few children.

Most of these private schools were held in the home of the teacher. They varied from cottages to quite large establishments. Presumably the teaching given therein varied similarly.

Though the essay deals with schools actually within the village of Cottingham, some details of other schools outside of the village but within the parish are necessary. In August, 1877 the National School at Newlands, which was then within the parish, was transferred to the Cottingham School Board and extensions added.

At a Board meeting in February, 1881, a letter was read from the Education Department approving plans for the erection of a Board School at Dunswell for 75 children and tenders were to be advertised. It was completed for opening on 7th November, 1881 and a mistress appointed at £60 per annum. The land for the school building cost two shillings and sixpence a square yard!

The Londesborough Street School was also the responsibility of the Cottingham Board and in fact employed a bigger staff than Newlands. It was transferred to the Hull Board in 1885 under the Hull Extension and Improvement Act of 1882 and renamed Lambert Street School.

The dissolution of the Cottingham School Board in 1903 marked the end of an era. The body set up to 'fill up gaps' absorbing as it did the functions of the other schools in the village was itself absorbed into an even bigger organisation, the East Riding Education Authority now itself engulfed in the even larger Humberside Education Authority. The period of the most dramatic increase in the population of the village occasioned the most ambitious schools building programme up to that date. In 1881 the population was 6,177. This rose to 10,103 by 1891, hence the necessity on the part of the School Board to acquire new premises to cater for the proportionate need for school places. The Boards were *ad hoc* authorities elected for the purposes of education only, with powers to borrow money for school building and to pre-empt on the rates. School provision was not balanced with the various other needs of an area such as roads, drains and so on, and therefore ambitious building projects could be embarked upon and the local Council or

Corporation had to foot the bill which brought forth cries of extravagance. In contrast, some areas saw little extra school provision; consequently both extremes helped to bring about the demise of the School Boards.

Cottingham Board provided according to its calculations, which were generous and far sighted at the time; the Boards were free of many of today's bureaucratic shackles and could therefore get on with the job of providing schools. It must be true to say that had too much restriction been put upon the powers of the Boards, there would not have been this burst of building energy and the subsequent increase in the number of schools available.

It is to the credit of the Cottingham Board that they, through their teachers, extended the curriculum to include topics not always associated with the functions of the School Boards, which were to provide elementary, i.e. basic, education; this was not a means to an end, a preparation for secondary education – it was an end in itself, a self-contained programme of education ceasing at eleven, twelve or thirteen years.

Today, in addition to the new Infant School erected on the site of the 19th century rectory, and the Junior Schools in Hallgate, three other Primary Schools in the area and the High School provide education for over 2,500 Cottingham children. Most of the old school buildings have now gone, with a few exceptions. The Mark Kirby School, Frances Coupland's little room close by, Eastholme College, and the School Board buildings, all serve as reminders of the pupils and their teachers in Cottingham schools during the 19th century.

BIBLIOGRAPHY

PRIMARY SOURCES

Cottingham Board School Minute Books, 1877-1892, 1892-1907.
Cottingham Boys' School Log Book.
Cottingham Girls' School Log Book.
Mark Kirby Charity Minute Book.
Archbishop Herring's Visitation Returns, York Diocese, 1743, Vol. I.
Baines, W., 1823 Yorkshire Directory, Vol. II, Hull, North and East Riding.
Kelly, R., 1893 Yorkshire Directory, North and East Ridings of Yorkshire.
White, W., 1831 Hull Directory.
White, W., 1840 Hull Directory.
White, F., 1858 Hull and District Directory.
White, F., 1867 Hull and District Directory.
Hull Advertiser; various dates from 1810-1901.
Population Census Returns 1801-1901.
Report of the Charity Commissioners: York City and East Riding, 1815-1830.
Report of Schools in Beverley Methodist Circuit Schedule 1: Day Schools.

SECONDARY SOURCES

A Short History of Cottingham. J. Whitehouse. The Parochial Church Council of St. Mary's
Church, Cottingham, 1974.
Church and People. St. Mary's Church Magazine, 1967.
Cottingham's Concern for its Poor to 1834. J. Whitehouse. Cottingham Local History
Society, 1970.
Cottingham Local History Society Journal, Vol. I, 1959-1964.
Cottingham Local History Society Journal, Vol. II, 1959-1964.
East Riding Deeds Registry, Beverley: copy of a letter loaned, referring to the Mark
Kirby buildings.
The National Society: documents and letters relating to the Mark Kirby Free School and
to the National Society.

APPENDIX

The population of Cottingham during the nineteenth century.

1801	—	1,927	1811	—	2,229	1821	—	2,479
1831	—	2,575	1841	—	2,618	1851	—	2,854
1861	—	3,140	1871	—	4,015	1881	—	6,177
1891	—	10,103	1901	—	16,987			